T0247238

GRIEF

REDEEMED

STEPHEN SILVER

GRIEF

REDEEMED

B&H
PUBLISHING
BRENTWOOD, TENNESSEE

9-798-3845-0124-4
Published by B&H Publishing Group
Brentwood, Tennessee

Dewey Decimal Classification: 155.9
Subject Heading: GRIEF / JOY AND SORROW /
BEREAVEMENT

Cover design by B&H Publishing Group.
Images by Irina Petrakova_6767/Shutterstock; LenLis /
Shutterstock. Author photo by Megan Farley.

1 2 3 4 5 • 27 26 25 24

Dedicated to the memory of Sandra Sweeny Silver

Now faith is the assurance of
things hoped for, the conviction
of things not seen.
Hebrews 11:1 ESV

For our light and momentary troubles
are achieving for us an eternal glory
that far outweighs them all. So we fix our
eyes not on what is seen, but on what is
unseen, since what is seen is temporary,
but what is unseen is eternal.
2 Corinthians 4:17–18

CONTENTS

Just three months before I said goodbye—for now—to my wife, Nanci, Steve Silver's wife, Sandy, went to be with Jesus. One day I didn't know Steve. The next, after a few hours talking together, I knew I'd found a good friend.

Twice he interviewed me about my grief journey and my final years with Nanci, and a deep bond was formed. In those interviews, Steve and I talked together about our dear wives, the present heaven they enjoy now, and the future heaven that God will bring down to the new earth, after the resurrection of all God's people.

Sandy and Nanci shared much in common, including their roles as our partners, soulmates, and best friends. Steve and I now share the common pilgrimage of grief, walking a path that, though full of learning and enrichment, is one we would gladly exchange to have our wives with us again. And yet . . . not really, because we both recognize God's sovereignty and love, and His perfect plan, and the fact that our wives are now happier than they have ever been.

Nanci experienced firsthand the closeness of Jesus in her suffering. She wrote in her journal, "My relationship with God has deepened more than I ever could have imagined during this cancer. I have tasted and seen that the Lord is good [Ps. 34:8]! I trust and cling to Him more. I worship Him more. I love Him more! The

Bible speaks to me more. The Holy Spirit's ministry feels more real to me."

I often picture Nanci's entry into Jesus's presence nearly a year ago. I imagine that while Jesus was both Sandy's and Nanci's center of attention, they also loved seeing relatives who had died—in Nanci's case, her mother and father and my parents, and our grandchild she'd not yet met, taken into heaven before birth. It makes me smile to think of Nanci and Sandy meeting each other in heaven and learning that their husbands are now friends.

As I told Steve, one of the truths I so love is that while Sandy and Nanci went ahead of us to the present pre-resurrection heaven, which is "better by far" than this earth under the curse, one day we will all be raised to life on the new earth. There, John says of our Lord, "He will wipe every tear from their eyes. There will be no more death or mourning or crying or pain, for the old order of things has passed away. He who was seated on the throne said, 'I am making everything new!' Then he said, 'Write this down, for these words are trustworthy and true'" (Rev. 21:4–5).

On that day, Sandy and Nanci and Steve and I—and all of God's risen people—will behold "the river of the water of life, as clear as crystal, flowing from the throne of God and of the Lamb down the middle of the great street of the city. On each side of the river stood the tree of life, bearing twelve crops of fruit, yielding its fruit every month. And the leaves of the tree are for the healing of the nations. No longer will there be any curse. The throne of God and of the Lamb will be in the city, and his servants will serve him. They will see his face . . ." (Rev. 22:1–4).

Can you imagine what it will be like for us all together—people of every tribe, nation, and language—to behold and experience at last the place that the Carpenter from Nazareth, infinitely creative and powerful, has prepared for us? Wow!

In this deeply personal and thoughtful book, *Grief Redeemed*, Steve Silver pours out his heart and tenderly examines aspects of his grief. He speaks of Sandy as his silent partner. He has "the memories of how Sandy would weigh in on decisions, encourage me in plans, guide me in right actions, and be an advocate for everything done for the Lord." I so relate. Nanci is my silent partner every day.

And yet in another way, she is not silent, nor is Sandy. Hebrews 11:4 says, "And by faith Abel still speaks, even though he is dead." Sandy and Nanci still speak to everyone who knew them here. And they speak to those they've been reunited with and have met for the first time. And they will forever speak, and one day we will hear not just memories of their voices, but their real present-tense voices, more delightful than ever.

I have written that grief has become my friend. When I saw Steve sharing the same—and also that grief was God's anvil to work on him—I recognized a common insight from the Holy Spirit. Neither of us asked grief to come into our lives because grief only comes with loss, and who asks for loss? But loss will come uninvited, and good grief can help us move forward through our losses, becoming more like Jesus in the process . . . if we let it.

"For our light and momentary troubles are achieving for us an eternal glory that far outweighs them all" (2 Cor. 4:17). Our deep pain in having to face this fallen world without our wives isn't just suffering for us to get beyond; it is suffering that is purposeful, achieving what's of eternal value. Because we know that, the next verse says, "So we fix our eyes not on what is seen, but on what is unseen. For what is seen is temporary, but what is unseen is eternal" (v. 18).

If your loved one has already died, I'm sure Steve's book will help you. If you or your spouse or a family member or close friend are dying, I hope this book will lead you to conversations about Jesus and the afterlife, and the need to prepare for it. I am so grateful that Nanci and I talked about heaven openly and often over decades, and I would encourage you to do the same.

Believing her death was coming soon, Nanci asked me if I would bring together our family of eleven—our two daughters and their husbands, and our five grandchildren. She wanted to speak into all our lives, and we gathered two days later. She spoke to her grandchildren especially, with tenderness and humor, and encouraged them never to resent God for taking her, because God always knows best and works even hard things for our eternal good. When she could speak no longer because of exhaustion, I read to the family from her journals. All of us were deeply touched. There were many tears, but also laughter, and it was Nanci's laughter that gave permission and blessing to ours.

One of our seventeen-year-old grandsons said, "Grams, if you can trust God like this when facing such hard things, I know I can trust Him too in the tough times I face." Another said, "I will never forget what you said to us today." We placed our hands on her and prayed over my wife, and our daughters' mother, and our grandsons' Gramma. It was a sacred time in which we caught glimpses of a far better world that she already had one foot in. What we experienced that day made me realize that none of us needs to wait until we think we're dying to gather and talk to our family as Nanci did. I've since encouraged others to consider doing this sooner rather than later.

Steve says that he didn't think much about heaven before Sandy went there. That changed everything for him, and he experienced a transformed perspective. I'd thought a great deal about heaven before Nanci died, having written seven books about it. But while what I learned during those hundreds (come to think of it, thousands) of hours spent on research and writing was a great encouragement, it didn't make saying good-bye to Nanci easy. All that study, however, bolstered my wholehearted belief that her death was not the end of our relationship, only a temporary interruption. The great reunion awaits us, and I anticipate it and delight in imagining it with everything in me.

Jesus kindly delivered Nanci and Sandy from their suffering. To know my sweetheart will never suffer another moment for all eternity brings tears of joy as I write these words.

When Nanci left for heaven, part of me left with her. Other than Jesus, the greatest treasure I've ever had on earth is Nanci. And Jesus said, "Where your treasure is, there your heart will be also." Because Jesus is in heaven, and He is my greatest treasure, my heart has long been there. But with Nanci there, as much as I love all my family and friends and church, my heart and mind are often in that other place. I'm encouraged by the command, "Set your hearts on things above, where Christ is, seated at the right hand of God. Set your minds on things above, not on earthly things" (Col. 3:1–2).

I'm grateful God still has a place for me as long as I'm here, just as Steve is finding the place God has for him. And, like Steve, I instinctively want to do things I would've done when Nanci was still here. One day somebody texted me a photo of their dog, and I immediately thought, I need to forward this to Nanci. Suddenly, the truth dawned on me: Nanci had been with Jesus ten months, yet my default inclination was still to send her that dog photo!

As Steve misses Sandy's daily presence, I find myself missing the thousands of little moments Nanci touched my life. Most of all I miss her laugh, which was frequent, loud, and contagious. She infused our home with happiness. I am still happy, but in Nanci's absence I find I need to be more deliberate in recounting all the reasons in Jesus that make me happy.

The time came, as it has for many others, when Nanci and I changed our prayers from "Lord, please heal Nanci" to "Lord, if You are not going to heal Nanci, please take her home soon."

With tears of joy and a love radiating from her eyes that I still see, she said to me, "Randy, thank you for my life!" Eyes full of tears, I said, "Nanci, thank you for my life!" Later, in her final days here in our earthly home, she said to me, "Randy, please take me Home." I said,

"If I could I would take you Home right now and I would never come back to this world the way it is."

I resonate when Steve says home for him was wherever Sandy was. It didn't matter where he was as long as she was there. Likewise, my house is less my home without Nanci, but heaven is more my home.

Steve realizes that his true home is where Jesus is. It warms my heart that Jesus and Sandy are in the same home. Nanci is with Jesus forever, and therefore, when the time comes for me to be with Jesus, it will mean being with Nanci. The two best friends I've ever had.

Nanci's final journal entry was, "I told the doctor today that I don't want to fight the cancer in order to just give me more time. I am going off chemo. I am so relieved and honestly excited! I will see Jesus pretty soon!!!" Exactly one month later, she did.

I often think of Nanci's reassurance to herself and to me: "God's got this! God's got me!" She wrote, "I will be ready to die when my time comes because my Shepherd will give me His joy, peace, and readiness. It will not be me working up enough faith and trust; my God will fight the battle for me! It will be His perfect ministering Spirit who will carry me peacefully—jubilantly—into God's arms."

I was a witness to the "peacefully" part as I watched her fall asleep, and then suddenly, I realized she'd stopped breathing, and, tears running down my face, I kissed her goodbye. Meanwhile, God, the angels, and likely some of heaven's inhabitants witnessed the "jubilantly" as they opened wide their arms and kissed her hello.

I have no doubt Nanci and Sandy both heard those words that should stir our hearts: "Well done, my good and faithful servant. Enter into your Master's happiness."

Sandy and Nanci were recipients of God's promise: "you will receive a rich welcome into the eternal kingdom of our Lord and Savior Jesus Christ" (2 Pet. 1:11). May each of us experience the same.

I pray each reader of this book will be drawn to Jesus, the Redeemer of Steve and Sandy, and Randy and Nanci, and all who place their trust in Him. He is the One who makes heaven such a wonderful place, all because He is such a wonderful person.

Randy Alcorn | March 2023
New York Times bestselling author of *Heaven*

I started this book of grief lessons in July 2022, seven months after my wife Sandy passed away. While it was a difficult period of grief, I knew I had to document what I was learning in my first year, so I began writing—one year after our 50th wedding anniversary.

Sandy fell in a parking lot in Naples on December 8, 2021, hitting her head hard on the pavement. I wasn't with her at the time but learned of her incident from the voicemail she left me:

> "Steve . . . I'm in trouble here in the hospital, I have bleeding in my brain, and I could die. Please, Honey, get here to the Naples Hospital emergency room as soon as you can for me. I love you, Honey. Bye Bye."

And so began this surreal period of my life.

I arrived in Sandy's emergency room, where she was awake (although heavily medicated), alert, and able to greet and visit with me. I was relieved that she wasn't in worse condition. I asked the ER physician how she was doing and was told "so far so good" because the bleeding had not yet penetrated the interior of her brain. They were monitoring for the possibility of that. Within a few minutes, she became disoriented and attempted to remove her intravenous tubes because they were uncomfortable.

As I left the room to get an ER nurse to help with the tubes, she leaned over the side of the bed and started vomiting—something I had never seen her do. I was advised this was an indication that the blood had entered the interior of her brain and was asked to leave while they went into triage mode. I had to sign papers authorizing emergency brain surgery (a craniotomy) to save her life.

I had called our three children while en route to the ER, and left voicemails that Mom was in trouble. By this time, they were all returning my calls and I patched us together by phone while in the ER waiting room so we could pray. We prayed for the neurosurgeon. We prayed Sandy would survive the surgery. We prayed for recovery and healing. We were all in this boat together with the Lord at the helm.

Sandy survived the surgery, in which they removed most of the blood to relieve pressure and allow her brain to come back into place within her skull. I met with her surgeon following the procedure and was told that her chances were 50/50 of waking up, and the same odds for survival if she did. There was nothing more to be done than watch, monitor, wait, pray, and trust the Lord with her outcome.

Two of our children flew down from New England the following morning and arrived in Sandy's critical care room that afternoon. Our third child arrived from California two days later and soon our whole family began the ensuing ten-day vigil with Sandy while her life weighed in the balance. Sandy was the glue of our family.

After thirteen days in and out of consciousness, some of which included seeing all of us at her bedside and heroically smiling and interacting with us as best she could in her badly weakened state, we were told that Sandy was not going to survive the sepsis condition that resulted from her lack of mobility. I'm certain she knew this as the final few days of her life drew to a close.

We had all asked the Lord and hoped for a miraculous recovery, but He chose instead to take her home with Him on December 21, 2021 at 1:10 p.m. We were all at her bedside playing the praise songs and Christmas carols she loved on a small Bluetooth speaker, reading Scripture to her, and telling her how much we loved her—something she told us daily. And so our much-beloved Sandy ended her life in her earthly body and began her eternal life in heaven.

Sandy's departure has been hard for me. She occupied so much of my life for so long, and our love and partnership were profound.

I read to her in the presence of our family at our 50th anniversary celebration in New Hampshire on July 1, 2021, just a few months earlier:

> There are so many things about being married to you that have changed, formed, and made life as I know it, there's not enough room here to enumerate them. I suppose I could sum it all up with this: My life began when I married you. I have no life apart from

you. All life centers around you. There truly is not, nor ever has been, anyone like you. You have taught me everything I know about love, kindness, and selflessness. I'm still amazed that you chose me. I guess this is where faith, grace, and marriage intersect. I can't separate them.

When I penned these words about a week before our 50th, I had no idea she would be gone six months later. If I had, I might have thought twice about saying "I have no life apart from you." However, that is what I believed and how I felt at the time. Over our fifty years together, I came to depend on Sandy's love, attention, support, encouragement, spiritual strength, and wisdom in ways beyond what might have been the case if she hadn't been such a life force on all those fronts. But she was, and anyone who knew her would agree. In retrospect, this was both a blessing and somewhat of a handicap for me.

I never saw the handicap part until she was no longer here. I had, in fact, become so reliant on her loving presence in my life that her absence from me now has been particularly difficult. I have effectively had to learn to function without her—a complete reorientation to a new normal I am trying to find, while constantly being reminded of her wherever I turn.

This, for me at least, is the essence of grieving—a long and arduous rehabilitation process. Not back to life as I once knew it but to a new life. One without Sandy but with memories of her and the best of what we built together. This is the journey I unexpectedly and reluctantly began.

From the sound of this, you might think that I have a dim and hopeless view of life on earth without Sandy, but that is not the case. In fact, I'm looking forward to the journey ahead, even knowing it will be scarred with sadness. This will be a different journey than the one I've been on with her these past fifty-one years. In a way, however, it will be an extension and completion of what we began together. For certain, Sandy will be a "silent partner" along the way. Let me explain.

I know that Sandy is not "with" me anymore. I don't think she's "looking out" for me, "helping" me, or even "encouraging" me from heaven. I simply have no biblical evidence for that, so I choose to look to the Lord, my earthly family, loved ones, close friends, and grief process guides for those roles. Thankfully, I am blessed with many of these people in my life.

What I mean by "silent partner" is the memories of how Sandy would weigh in on decisions, encourage me in plans, guide me in right actions, and be an advocate for everything done for the Lord. Sandy was my ballast whenever I would careen in the wrong direction or get out of balance. She was a predictable and dependable barometer of the Lord to get me back on keel when I would wander off course—which I frequently did.

Because of thousands of iterations of that over the years, I became a better man with her partnership and am equipped to finish well without her daily reminders. I will look to the Lord for those now, but the memories of "Sandy Wisdom" will always serve me well.

I used to say that my marriage was the anvil on which the Lord was forging the new man in Christ that He was fashioning for His purposes on this side of heaven. I now believe that my grief is His new anvil for me, and that the lessons I learn in grief will have redemptive value well beyond this difficult period—however long that lasts.

This journal captures the hopeful lessons I've learned about grief during the first eighteen months since Sandy's death. They have served as helpful guides for navigating my new life here without her and will hopefully be of some help to you—my grief sojourner.

We share the common experience of a painful loss of a loved one. Those who haven't walked in our shoes are able to understand our grief—and even with that understanding, none of us experience it the same. However, there are similarities in our experience—landmarks, so to speak, which you will recognize and with which you will be able to identify.

Your loss may be very recent, or you may be further along in your process. In reading these lessons, you will see a positive progression in my experience. The early lessons reflect more visceral pain than later ones. My disposition gets lighter, joy prevails over sadness, and my outlook for the future brightens. Depending on how early you are in your grief process, you may not be able to relate to my later lessons as well as the earlier ones.

However, I can assure you that your pain will lighten over time and that you, like me, will eventually be able to embrace your future with hope, purpose, and fulfillment. Your sadness will turn to sweet, cherished memories of your loved one and your tears of anguish will turn to tears of joy—"Weeping may endure for a night, But joy comes in the morning" (Ps. 30:5 NKJV).

Thank you for sharing this journey with me.

Stephen Silver

GRIEF IS NOT MY ENEMY

I've learned that grief is not my enemy—it is my friend. This insight hasn't mitigated or softened the pain of Sandy's absence from me, nor the loneliness and emptiness I experience every day when reflecting on her love, friendship, companionship, support, encouragement, and beautiful smile. However, I've discovered that the more visceral these feelings, the greater the opportunity to draw closer to the Lord in the midst of my anguish. I've learned that in those moments, He has me exactly where He wants me—pouring out my heart and tears before Him and asking for His help to get me through.

The truth is, I've never experienced real suffering before—not on this level. Like everyone, I've had normal disappointments, regrets, and life challenges with which I've had to cope. But none of those came close to the heartache and pain of the reality of no longer having Sandy by my side or seeing her face again in this life. There's simply no way to sugarcoat or dodge those realizations and related emotions when they come crashing in.

As with most who've experienced heavy grief from loss, these come upon me in the form of giant waves which capsize and render me momentarily incapaci-tated. In the first few months after Sandy's death, these came frequently and without warning. All I could do was hold on until they passed, or sometimes call a close family member or friend to help me get through them. Fortunately, these now come less frequently, are less intense, and don't last as long—but I know they are coming.

Until recently, I saw these "grief waves" as unwel-come but unavoidable enemies to be endured until they let me out of their clutches. That may be because I didn't know how deep they would cut, or how to manage them when they showed up. I now have more experience with them and have come to understand that they are not my enemies at all but, as I have said, are indeed my friends.

There's no way to rationalize away the profound sadness of missing the presence of someone you deeply loved and on who's special closeness you came to depend. *Dependence* entails counting on the certain and confident knowledge that they will always be there—across the dinner or card table, in the car seat next to you, on the couch watching a movie, in the bed beside you, holding your hand, calling on the phone . . . the list goes on. These are thousands of daily touch points that make up life together and became as natural and neces-sary as breathing.

When these are all removed at the passing of your loved one, but the memories of them persist, their absence can be heart wrenching and you would give anything to experience again any of what you proba-bly once took for granted. Fortunately, time and new experiences have a way of taking over those "touch points" and replacing them with a new normal—but there are those memories, and something needs to be done with them when they come.

So why would you welcome memories which only make you sad? How could they be your friends? Wouldn't it be better to be free and clear of them? Logic would seem to argue the case for pressing the sad memories delete button. Simple as that. But let's explore that option.

What if you could do it? Wave your hand and be 100 percent clear of all memories of your loved one? What would you gain? You may be a happier person. You wouldn't be sideswiped by the pangs of sadness that come over you throughout the day. Crying would no longer be as frequent for you, nor loom below the surface of conversations when in the company of friends and family. You would likely be easier to be around. You could get on with your new life more quickly and have a nice spring in your step. But what would you lose?

I can only speak for myself here. For me, I would lose the opportunity to become a better man and more useful instrument for the Lord. The sadness I experience in grief over memories of Sandy is the raw material, so to speak, that the Lord has been using to draw me closer to Him—closer than I would have ever been able to be without the grief. It is breaking down my self-reliance, increasing my dependence on Him, and making me more vulnerable to others. It is softening me, making me more tenderhearted, sensitive to others, and interested in their lives. In short, it is making me more accessible and less self-centered.

When I am particularly missing Sandy and the tears come, they are now a form of soul-cleansing that somehow make me feel renewed, refreshed, and better equipped for the day. The pain of missing Sandy is still acute, and I find myself loving her more each day. However, I think I've turned the corner of "needing" and depending on her, to being thankful for what I had with her here for more than fifty years, rejoicing in her present fullness in heaven, looking forward to our reunion there, and embracing what the Lord has left for me to do here in my "new and improved" state.

I ask myself, given the choice, if I would turn back the clock and change the circumstances of her death to have her back with me to pick up where we left off before her fall—and my answer is *no*, I wouldn't. Her life has improved exponentially being in heaven, and I wouldn't want to deprive her of that; and the grief I've acquired through her absence will now be my new companion and tutor for a life I wasn't planning or welcoming but that the Lord has chosen as His plan for me.

So yes, grief is my friend.

Questions for Reflection

1. Have you found unexpected closeness to the Lord and comfort from Him in pouring out your heart and tears to Him in your deepest moments of sadness? If so, you understand this silver lining in grief. If not, why do you think you have been holding yourself back from Him?

2. It's easy to get trapped in the feeling of wishing things could go back to the way it was. If you were able to miraculously have that, what would you gain and what would you lose?

"BLESSED ARE THOSE WHO MOURN, FOR THEY WILL BE COMFORTED." (MATT. 5:4)

HEAVEN IS OUR COMMON HOME

On the six-month anniversary of Sandy's death, after being in the final earthly home we owned together for only a year, I decided it was time to sell the house and I wrote this to our children:

> While the last year here was brief, in certain ways it was one of the most special. Perhaps it's because on some level we knew it would be our good-bye home—the culmination of twelve moves from Edinburgh to Bethel. These homes were where we started and built our life and family together. We finished in Naples on 12/21/21, but still have a final home in heaven to inhabit together. She has just gone ahead of me by a few years. Home was wherever Sandy was. The location didn't matter to me as long as she was there. She always made me feel safe, loved, appreciated, and cherished. She was the ultimate homemaker.

Life with Sandy, imbued with the love of Christ which spilled over to our family and close friendships, had become my center of gravity. I was comfortable, happy, at peace, and blessed. I knew that and was very thankful for the life we were living together. Sandy was too. We would regularly weigh-in about how blessed our lives were. We were content to enjoy our golden years until one of us would eventually leave—a thought that rarely entered our minds since we were both in good health, functioning on most cylinders, and chose to avoid that subject.

I used to jokingly say that we would go together—not by a traumatic incident but by passing away together in our sleep. Perhaps that's because the alternative of one being left alone without the other was too unthinkable.

I admit that I didn't think much about heaven before Sandy relocated there.

Her death changed everything.

It changed my paradigm about the tenuousness and relative brevity of life here. It changed my desire for many more years here. And it changed how I intend to spend my remaining time.

Home is wherever Sandy is—and her home is now in heaven. From the moment she arrived there, I became laser beam–focused on learning all I could about her new address. I wanted, with any credible resources available and as much as humanly possible, to be able to envision her new life there. That's because I wasn't ready to be separated from "home." I had (and still have) a thousand questions, most of which won't be fully answered until I get there. To name just a few:

How is she spending her time?

Who is she visiting with?

Is she still the voracious knowledge seeker and disseminator she was here?

Has she gotten answers to her questions?

Is she able to share knowledge, something she loved to do?

Does she still look like Sandy?

Does she think about and miss us in ways similar to how we remember, think about, and miss her?

What will our reunion be like when it's my time to leave for heaven?

If there's no longer marriage in heaven, what form will the love and union we built here take on?

How will our relationship change?

Will it be as unique and special as it was here?

Pondering questions like these about my future home and her current one help me stay connected to her. They seem to bridge the gap between us and alleviate the severity of missing her. I think that's "admissible" in a healthy grieving process. If these were to over occupy my daily thoughts, if I were to attempt ways of trying to communicate with her or adopt non-biblically supported answers—that would become unhealthy. However, knowing that heaven is our final common home, and that she simply got there a few years before me, it seems natural and fitting to explore that territory with Sandy in mind.

I have used several biblically based resources to assist me in this exploration. These include Randy Alcorn's *Heaven*, Dr. David Jeremiah's *Answers to Your Questions about Heaven*, Dr. Robert Jeffress's *A Place Called Heaven*, and Richard Baxter's classic *The Saints' Everlasting Rest* (written in 1650). I'm sure there are others that I will read at some point, but these have given me a good perspective and meet my needs for the time being, and I would recommend them to you as well.

When I looked at Randy Alcorn's table of contents in his masterful book *Heaven*, I immediately honed in on "Chapter 35: Will There Be Marriage, Families, and Friendships?" I decided to start there. Here's part of what Randy says about marriage in heaven:

> Here on earth we long for perfect marriage. That's exactly what we'll have—a perfect marriage with Christ. My wife, Nanci, is my best friend and my closest sister in Christ. Will we become more distant in the new world? Of course not—we'll become

closer, I'm convinced. The God who said "it is not good for the man to be alone" (Genesis 2:18) is the giver and blesser of our relationships. Life on this earth matters. What we do here touches strings that reverberate for all eternity. Nothing will take away the fact that Nanci and I are marriage partners here and that we invest so much of our lives in each other, serving Christ together. I fully expect no one besides God will understand me better on the New Earth [heaven], and there's nobody whose company I'll seek and enjoy more than Nanci's.

The joys of marriage will be far greater because of the character and love of our bridegroom. I rejoice for Nanci and me that we'll both be married to the most wonderful person in the universe. He's already the one we love most—there's no competition. On Earth, the closer we draw to him, the closer we draw to each other. Surely the same will be true in Heaven. What an honor it will be to always know that God chose us for each other on this old Earth so that we might have a foretaste of life with him on the New Earth. People with good marriages are each other's best friends. There's no

> reason to believe they won't still be
> best friends in Heaven.[1]

When I read this, I took it to the bank. It made total sense and didn't seem to conflict with Scripture. For me, it has become a level-set on how to think about my relationship with Sandy in heaven. Since her absence from me here has been so surreal, I had to grasp the reality of my future with her there, and this is a plausible and biblically supportable one—so it's good enough for me.

I have to admit that, unlike the case with Randy, I cannot honestly say that I loved the Lord more than Sandy when she was alive—that there was "no competition." In fact, there was with me. I know there wasn't for her. He was her first love, more than me or our children and grandchildren. I knew and loved that about her, and never considered competing with Him for her love and devotion. I knew that the closer she was to Him, the more she would love me and the more fulfilled I'd be because of that. In hindsight, I believe I experienced Christ's love so much through her that I wasn't compelled to pursue a closer relationship with Him apart from her.

This has no longer been the case since her passing into heaven. I now come before and look mainly to Him for comfort, consolation, wisdom, and guidance— something I regularly did with Sandy. I jokingly (yet honestly) say that Sandy is the first person I'll want to see when I get to heaven. But I believe, based on my current trajectory of intimacy with the Lord, that He will be the first person I want to see when I finally get there—at least I hope so.

Nanci Alcorn passed away on March 28, 2022 (eighteen years after Randy published *Heaven*) following a long battle with colon cancer. Upon her passing Randy wrote:

> Nanci is with Jesus. So happy for her. Sad for us. But the happiness triumphs over the sadness. Grieving is ahead, and it will be hard, but these last years and especially this last month have given us a head start on the grieving process. I am so proud of my wife for her dependence on Jesus and her absolute trust in the sovereign plan and love of God.[2]

I'm certain Randy's priorities with Jesus were well in order before Nanci's passing into heaven, and I look forward to hearing from him about how he's handling their temporary separation.

In his book, *A Place Called Heaven*, Dr. Robert Jeffress says:

> Heaven is the promise that God will eventually make all things right and that He will one day fulfill our deepest longings. Although God's promise is yet future, it should make a tremendous difference in our lives today. As Alcorn explained, "If we grasp it, [heaven] will shift our center of gravity

and radically change our perspective on life."[3]

Thoughts about and the pursuit of heaven, even if instigated by Sandy's going there, have changed my "center of gravity." It has shifted from Sandy to striving toward the goal and prize of my heavenly home. In short, I have become heavenly minded—and that is a good thing. It took the reality of living out the rest of my life here without her to look upon every day as one closer to reaching heaven in a way that will be pleasing to the Lord. Saint Paul had this perspective, which I always loved but have now come to understand on a more personal level:

> I want to know Christ—yes, to know the power of his resurrection and participation in his sufferings, becoming like him in his death, and so, somehow, attaining to the resurrection from the dead. Not that I have already obtained all this, or have already arrived at my goal, but I press on to take hold of that for which Christ Jesus took hold of me. Brothers and sisters, I do not consider myself yet to have taken hold of it. But one thing I do: Forgetting what is behind and straining toward what is ahead, I press on toward the goal to win the prize for which God has called me heavenward in Christ Jesus. (Phil. 3:10–14)

If it sounds as if my newfound focus on heaven is motivated by attempts to apprehend Sandy's life there, and take comfort in my eventual reunion with her, well—it is. I understand that this is not the primary mindset I should ultimately have about heaven and am certain I will mature beyond this over time, but I also know that God knows the truth about where I am and where I am going and will continue to lead me down the path into His arms.

I have found this to be helpful on the path of grief. When I become acutely aware of her absence from me, and the waves of pain roll in, I fix my mind on the joyful existence she is now living and my tears of sadness become commingled with tears of joy—joy for the eternal life she has inherited, for the one I'm headed toward, and for the hope and promise of a purposeful finishing chapter here.

Questions for Reflection

1. Do you find yourself thinking more about heaven, and your loved one's new life there? Have you found that makes your grief easier to deal with?

2. How does focusing on your final home in heaven change the way you see your current life here?

3. What should you change in your life to show that you are living more heavenly minded?

BROTHERS AND SISTERS, I DO NOT CON-
SIDER MYSELF TO HAVE TAKEN HOLD OF IT.
BUT ONE THING I DO: FORGETTING WHAT IS
BEHIND AND REACHING FORWARD TO WHAT
IS AHEAD, I PURSUE AS MY GOAL THE PRIZE
PROMISED BY GOD'S HEAVENLY CALL IN
CHRIST JESUS. (PHIL. 3:13–14 csb)

REALITY IS LIBERATING

One of my biggest struggles has been accepting the reality of Sandy's absence. Of course, I know she is gone and that I won't see her again here. However, the strong memories of her create an illusion of her presence. I hear her voice. I see her sitting at the table. I feel her embrace. I sense her love and affection toward me. These moments can seem so real that I want to (and sometimes do) speak to her out loud, reach for her hand, take out my phone to call her, and in other ways attempt to bridge her relocation to heaven.

I know that these are only memory fragments of the lifetime Sandy and I spent together. It's hard adapting to a new reality when the former one is comprised of millions of sweet experiences and exchanges that made up more than two-thirds of my life. So what does one do? For me, it comes down to acceptance. Accepting the unalterable fact that Sandy is no longer here.

She isn't in bed beside me when I wake up. She isn't at home to call and ask to meet me outside for an afternoon drive. She isn't there to read my little love note texts to her throughout the day, nor to write them to me. If I look her up on my Find My Friends app (which

I occasionally still do), I see "Location Not Found" because heaven is not trackable. She won't be sending me her monthly blog articles to edit. She isn't there to comment on and edit my writing.

When it's our regular afternoon or evening time to play our running games of Canasta or Spades (where "all the problems of the world are suspended" as we used to say), she isn't there to shuffle the cards, keep score, and forget who won the last game—because it didn't matter. She won't be there to go with me to the airport to pick up our children and grandchildren when they come to visit. She won't be there to go to McDonald's or Wendy's for lunch, and sit in the parking lot to listen to talk radio and discuss current events—something we did several days a week. She won't be there to plan and take getaway weekends. She won't be there for long backroad drives throughout our beloved Vermont— something she did with me because she knew I loved them. She won't be there to help me plan and organize our next big anniversary trip, which we did every five years.

I could go on and on. These are just a snapshot of the "millions of sweet experiences and exchanges" that I took for granted in real time, and now would give anything to relive just one. Perhaps that's one of the advantages of loss—their absence makes one appreciate them that much more. Appreciation is a wonderful thing. They say that "absence makes the heart grow fonder." I'm finding this to be true.

When I reflect on these times that comprised life with Sandy, they all bring me to tears—tears of sorrow over their loss, but also tears of joy and appreciation for their permanent place in my heart. While we will no longer be able to build more of these together on earth, the reality of their place in our life together here is undeniable and unshakable. Not only will I not try to escape them to make life without her more tolerable, but rather I will incorporate them into my remaining years here—thereby remaining united with her in memory and incorporating the best of who we were together into the newly fashioned man I am becoming.

The man I became with more than fifty years of "two becoming one" with Sandy, knitted together in Christ, is far better than the man I was before, and the Lord is not finished with me yet. In fact, as I have already stated, He is using my grief as the anvil for His continued work in me. Our daughter Kathy, also a widow, says: "I'm sad to the core but broken to my advantage." I so admired her when she said that following her husband Walt's untimely death five years ago. I now know exactly what she meant.

The tricky part for me going forward, and what I need to be cautious of, is the potential of conflating memories of these past experiences with an illusion of Sandy's continued presence with me in spirit here on earth. I'm certain Sandy is no longer here on any level and is fully engaged in heaven. When I talk to her out loud (which I still occasionally do), it is for my comfort and benefit, and not because I expect her to hear or respond to me. When I sense her love, I believe it is a lovely memory of her and the Lord's actual loving presence wrapped in that memory.

While it's true that I experienced the Lord's love for me through Sandy on earth, I believe that ceased when she went to heaven. However, the Lord's presence didn't leave me when she did. He remains and His love is always with me. Reality for me is knowing that when my love for Sandy is at times so strong that it pours out of me in ways I can't contain, that the Lord is wrapped in that love and pouring it right back into me. At those times, which are currently coming more frequently, I find myself telling Sandy out loud how much I love her and simultaneously asking the Lord to tell her for me—and it is then that I experience the Lord's love for me most intimately.

Last night, while sitting on our patio watching one of the August sunsets like Sandy and I used to do, I had one of those moments. My love for her was so overpowering, I asked the Lord what to do with it? What I felt I heard back was: *Give it to Me—Give it to her—Give it to others.* That was wise instruction and immediately reminded me of what I had read a few days ago in Martha W. Hickman's beautiful daily devotional, *Healing After Loss*, which has been so helpful to me:

> Of course we miss the expressions of love from the one we have lost. And our love for that person, too, goes on and on. Where can we put it? We direct it into the air, hoping somehow it will find its target.
>
> Things could be worse! Imagine what it would be like if, in our grieving, not only were we unable to love the one who is gone, but we couldn't

respond with overflowing hearts to the
dear ones who come to comfort us.

Music has been called a universal
language. Love is another. But it takes
constant replenishment, and fortunate
are we if our experience has been such
that we can be among the replenishers
of that love.[4]

This is all a mysterious phenomenon that I don't fully
understand, and that Martha does a better job than I of
describing. Suffice it to say that the lens I am adopting
is one of Sandy's full life now in heaven, mine here with
real and permanent memories of her, and the Lord's
love equally present in both places. I don't need the
illusion of Sandy's continued presence with me here to
give me the strength I need for the journey ahead. The
sweet memories of fifty-one years of life with her here,
the knowledge that I will see her again, and the Lord's
love and guidance in my remaining years—is more than
sufficient. This reality is liberating. Tim Keller, quoting
a sermon outline from Jonathan Edwards, says it well:

Our bad things will turn out for good
(Rom. 8:28), Our good things can
never be taken away from us (Ps.
4:6–7), and the best things are yet to
come (1 Cor. 2:9).[5]

Questions for Reflection

1. When do you find yourself struggling with the reality of the loss of your loved one?

2. How do you see yourself trying to escape memories of your loved one in order to make life without them more tolerable?

3. How have you been able to incorporate sweet memories of the life you had with your loved one into the one you now have without them? The best of who you were together into the newly fashioned person you are becoming?

"SO YOU ALSO HAVE SORROW NOW. BUT I WILL SEE YOU AGAIN. YOUR HEARTS WILL REJOICE, AND NO ONE WILL TAKE AWAY YOUR JOY FROM YOU." (JOHN 16:22 csb)

ONLY A BREATH AWAY

While I have come to accept the reality of Sandy's absence from me until our reunion in heaven and have no illusions about my ability to somehow connect with her in the interim, I do believe she is only a breath away—just beyond the veil between love here and love in heaven. That is the same love, the same formulation, created and sustained by the Lord, who's nature is constant and immutable here and in heaven.

When I am pierced with memories of Sandy, I find what helps me through is to close my eyes and fall into the Lord's loving arms through tears of brokenness. In that place I somehow feel suspended between heaven and earth. It's a place I didn't experience before Sandy's death and for which I'm grateful. While I can't experience Sandy's presence in that state, I know that I am experiencing a thimble-sized portion of the same love she is experiencing in abundance at that same moment. The same Lord, the same love—not an earth version and a heaven version, but the same one experienced in different portions. I find that comforting.

Martha W. Hickman speaks to this in reflecting on the death of their daughter in *Healing After Loss*:

What we have lost is not replaceable—
is not supplanted by the other mani-
festations of life around us, no matter
how beautiful—any more than the loss
of a child is made up for by the birth
of another child. And yet . . . and yet
. . . perhaps it can give us comfort to
think about the oneness of creation.
The words on a poster our daughter
had hung in her room shortly before
her death began, "the same sun warms
us," and went on to say, ". . . and we
share each other's lives, lingering in
each other's shadows." My husband
and I framed the poster, and for many
years it hung in my writing room—a
source of great comfort.[6]

"Lingering in each other's shadows." I love that
image. So near and yet so inaccessible. For me, the
nearness of our common experience of Christ's love
softens the hardship of not having her here by my side.
I deeply miss her presence and always will (I'm resolved
to this), but I know she is only a breath away. My last
breath, whenever that comes, will instantly usher me
into the Lord's presence, my ultimate home, and where
she already dwells. I can live with that. In fact, I rejoice
in the promise of that. In the meantime, while still here,
Martha W. Hickman expresses beautifully,

Maybe such a journey of faith is a bit
like walking toward home in the dark.
There is no light to see by, but we

grope our way in this familiar yet unfa-
miliar world, turning where we know
the road turns, moving toward what we
know must be there. Though we can't
see ahead, the ground beneath our feet
seems right, and as we approach a door
that surely must be there, somebody
inside, somebody we love, turns on the
light to welcome us home.[7]

For those who have put their hope in Christ, while we
see through a glass darkly here—we do see. We glimpse
our future home. We imagine our loved one there, so full
of life and joy. We worship and follow the same Lord and
Shepherd, and He calls us both by name. While Sandy
was my wife here, she was also my sister in Christ—and
still is. While I'm not yet able to fellowship with her in
heaven, I know I will be doing so soon enough. I also
know that we are members of the same body of Christ—
His church, His bride, His congregation united in sing-
ing praises to Him. While Sandy wasn't much of a singer
here, her heart could rejoice in abandoned praise like few
I've ever known. I imagine her doing that now, with her
beautiful smile and a newfound sweet and melodious
voice. I cherish that picture.

"If then you were raised with Christ, seek those
things which are above, where Christ is, sitting at the
right hand of God. Set your mind on things above, not
on things on the earth. For you died, and your life is
hidden with Christ in God. When Christ who is our life
appears, then you will appear with Him in glory" (Col.
3:1–4 NKJV).

Questions for Reflection

1. Knowing that you are experiencing the same immutable love of Christ on earth as your loved one is experiencing in heaven, in what ways does that bring you comfort?

2. Martha W. Hickman refers to the veil between our life here and our loved one's life in heaven as "lingering in each other's shadows." Knowing that you are not actually communicating, have you ever sensed an otherwise inexplicable "so near and yet so inaccessible" closeness?

FOR NOW WE SEE ONLY A REFLECTION AS IN A MIRROR, BUT THEN FACE TO FACE. NOW I KNOW IN PART, BUT THEN I WILL KNOW FULLY, AS I AM FULLY KNOWN. (1 COR. 13:12 csb)

MY FUTURE BECKONS

My approach to this book has been to wait for new lessons from my grieving process to develop and present themselves. I don't force them out before their time but let them have their own voice. Any other approach could produce premature or half-baked insights or, worse, lessons that won't have lasting life application.

I have been spending time alone in our Vermont house. The last time I did this, over a month ago, I was unable to enjoy the beauty of our home because everywhere I looked I was reminded of Sandy's absence. I told my family that I no longer wanted to be there alone, because it was too difficult. Then I decided to give it another try. I'm glad I did.

When I look around the rooms at all the country furniture, wall art, photos, antiques, books, knickknacks, throw blankets, personalized saying signs, and everything else we've collected over thirty years—I'm struck by what a wonderful home Sandy and I have created and curated, and by how much it reflects her unique and eclectic personality. Rather than being unbearably sad and wanting to leave when I look around, I smile and remember.

I remember when we first walked into the house with our realtor after Christmas in 1992, saw the long mountain views from the large picture windows, toured the house with delight as we entered each room, imagined ourselves living here, and gave each other knowing glances of approval. We knew we had found the Vermont mountain retreat we had been looking for.

I remember Sandy creating the color schemes she would use when decorating. I remember picking out furniture and antiques to add character and "anchor" the house, as she called it. I remember shopping for Vermont-made accessories and nonperishable food items to fill out open cabinets. I remember going to galleries throughout Vermont to find just the right country prints and photographs and placing them just so.

I remember lying on a blanket in the backyard at night, holding hands, gazing at the stars, and being amazed at how clear and perfect they looked. I remember New Year's Eve celebrations over the years where our sons and their friends would put on fireworks displays in the back field at our annual gatherings that would rival any small town's. I remember Sandy's pork, sauerkraut, and mashed potato dinners served at 11:00 p.m. following the fireworks—and how the doors would need to be left open, no matter how cold, to let out the smells and smoke from frying pork.

I could go on about how much Sandy and I loved this home together, incorporated our family and extended family into our special world, and how much it has come to mean to all of us. In short, it embodies family more than any other place. And here's the rub—Sandy was our curator and glue. Without consciously trying and certainly without taking credit, Sandy was the primary creator and central soul of this place. Everyone would agree with that. Perhaps that explains my visceral reaction during my last visit. The remembrances of her here were too hard to handle. Rather than embracing the memories, I rejected the house and wrote it off as no longer a viable part of my future.

I'm glad I returned and have had a 180-degree shift in my disposition. All those memories are now sweet rather than bitter. While Sandy is no longer here physically, she is inextricably woven into the fabric and history of this home and always will be. What was I thinking? How could I have been on the verge of rejecting this wonderful part of our life and family history? What was going on inside of me? I believe the answer is simple—the pain of loss clouded the beauty and joy of memories. In the short period of time between visits here, something changed inside of me, and now I love and look forward to being here alone or with family and friends.

This change is only one manifestation of the larger lesson now presenting itself, that my future beckons me. Until this trip, Vermont would no longer be a substantive part of my future. I wouldn't have sold the house, which would have broken my family's hearts, but I wouldn't have come unless they were here. Now I will. Why is this important? Because my future in this life no longer entails Sandy occupying it with me. Whatever it is, it won't include her beyond the memories of her—and those will take an appropriate place.

I will embrace every facet of my new life, whether or not Sandy was a former part of it, with anticipation and excitement. If she was a part of it before, the memories of her in those contexts will be wonderful. If she wasn't, they will become new experiences with new memories to be formed. This is a meaningful paradigm shift as I enter the ninth month since Sandy's passing. I now find myself thinking as much about my new future without her as my past life with her.

Part of me feels guilty about this, as if I'm somehow being disloyal to the memory of her by being happy and excited about my future. However, I know that guilt doesn't come from a healthy place and that Sandy would be rooting for me to embrace my future—especially since she knows the Lord is the One guiding it.

While the specifics of my future have yet to be fleshed out, the framework seems to be up. I like what I see and am excited to watch the house come together. I'm particularly enthused about my contractor, the Lord, who designed the blueprints and is overseeing the construction. That is the best part. It's not necessary here to describe the framework of my future. Suffice it to say, it's a logical extension of the life I built with the Lord and Sandy since meeting both of them in 1970, the man I became during those fifty-one years, and the talents and gifts with which the Lord has equipped me. The future beckons, and I'm looking forward to it.

Questions for Reflection

1. Are there some places or activities that you are avoiding because they still feel too difficult?

2. Are you able to glimpse a future for yourself, without your loved one, which you can look forward to—and perhaps even become excited about? What does that life look like?

"FOR I KNOW THE PLANS I HAVE FOR YOU"—THIS IS THE Lord'S DECLARA-TION—"PLANS FOR YOUR WELL-BEING, NOT FOR DISASTER, TO GIVE YOU A FUTURE AND A HOPE." (JER. 29:11 csb)

HOME IS WHERE THE LORD IS

In Lesson Two of this journal I shared a note that I sent to our three children on the six-month anniversary of Sandy's death. In part of it I said:

> Home was wherever Sandy was. The location didn't matter to me as long as she was there. She always made me feel safe, loved, appreciated, and cherished. She was the ultimate homemaker.

This strong identification with Sandy as home was one of the most powerful and poignant aspects of our life together. She truly was home base. No matter where I was or what I was doing while away from the house—whether on a business trip, playing golf with friends, doing errands, or anything else—I always knew she would likely be researching or writing at her computer or close by if she was out and about.

When I called, she'd answer on the first or second ring. When I texted or emailed, she'd reply within minutes. When I'd pull up to the garage, her bright red VW bug would usually be in its spot. When I'd walk in the door, I could count on her to stop whatever she was doing to greet me with a warm hug and a kiss and tell me about what she was working on. The few times she wasn't there when I got home, I might even go looking for her car (so easy to spot) in one of her usual shopping or lunch spots—and seek her out to surprise her.

Yes, we were that joined at the hip. I could count on my "Sandy home base" as surely as the sun rising and setting in the morning and evening. This was a sure thing and comforting me throughout my days. There aren't many of those in life. Although she never expressed this and was a bit more independent, I believe she felt the same toward me. If I had to say what I miss most about Sandy's departure to heaven, it's this reliance and assurance that she would always be there for me.

Even after nine months, I'm having trouble accepting that I can no longer count on what had become such a predictable, stabilizing, and joyful foundation in my life. While she was here, I couldn't imagine the possibility of a time when this would not be the case, and certainly never pondered an alternative reality. And yet, here I am.

A few days ago I was on my way home from some errands and was struck with excitement and joy over her greeting me when I'd walk in the door. That's a feeling that would often precede getting home to her. This day was an instinctive response to a former pattern. Without knowing it, I momentarily forgot she wouldn't be there. That only lasted a second before realizing that my earthly home was no longer a place that Sandy inhabited. That was hard. Then within seconds I had a wonderful, joyful insight—home with Sandy was now being replaced by home with the Lord. Home would no longer be wherever Sandy was, it would be wherever the Lord is.

I closed on the sale of the home to which I referred in one of the early lessons—the last home we bought before her passing. We were only there a little over a year and had just finished decorating and settling in. We had envisioned that being our final Northern home together, and indeed it was. I thought we'd have more years to enjoy it but am grateful for the brief time we had there.

As the movers were packing everything up the day before the closing, I sat in a chair watching and reflecting upon how soon after moving in it was now being dismantled. It felt like a metaphor for my life—what I have known and counted on with Sandy was now being dismantled. Only nine months ago we were completing final decorating, playing spades at our dining room table, planning what we'd do that day, and enjoying a late summer/early fall day together. Fortunately, I had no clue that two months later I'd receive a call from Sandy in the ER. James says it well:

> You do not know what tomorrow will
> bring. What is your life? For you are a
> mist that appears for a little time and
> then vanishes. (James 4:14 ESV)

As I drove away from the house after turning over the keys to the new owners, I knew that a door was closing—the door of our final home together this side of heaven. There will be other homes I'll inhabit alone, including two we've owned and enjoyed together for nearly thirty years and that I don't intend to sell. But this one is somehow different. While I can't fully explain it, this change had a punctuated finality to it. This really was goodbye.

While I no longer feel as adrift as I did in the early months since Sandy's departure, I still don't completely have my footing. For me, "footing" equates to that "home base" to which I referred. No person on earth will ever again be "home base" for me as Sandy was. I know that and won't try to cling to a home base that no longer exists.

The challenge ahead, and it is still a challenge at this point, is in transitioning from home is where Sandy is— to home is where the Lord is. I've begun that quest and am confident, as long as I continue to look ahead and trust Him, that the Lord will guide me to that place. I know for certain that is where Sandy is now and that she would want this for me.

Questions for Reflection

1. What do you now consider to be home base? Has that changed since the loss of your loved one?

2. Have there been moments since losing your loved one that felt like closing a door? Or thoughts you need to adopt in order to walk through the new door of your future home?

3. Have you been able thus far to transition from "home is where your loved one is" to "home is where the Lord is?" How is that manifesting itself in your day-to-day life?

"IF I GO AWAY AND PREPARE A PLACE FOR YOU, I WILL COME AGAIN AND TAKE YOU TO MYSELF, SO THAT WHERE I AM YOU MAY BE ALSO." (JOHN 14:3 CSB)

MY NEW COUNTRY

For a while we are so infused with grief over our loss that we can think of little else. Everything else seems an intrusion. If people call us on other matters we think, "Don't you know there isn't space in my life for that right now?"

But grieving can be habit-forming, and after a while we need to move on. Retreat into our own small world and its painful security will not protect us from further dangers. But it may keep us from savoring the world—its beauties and relationships, which are also passing, and which our loved one would want us to enjoy to the full.[8]

The other night, while watching a movie at our son's house, I was suddenly hit in the gut with an overwhelming wave of missing Sandy. *She should be here with me*, I thought. *This is too hard.* I thought I was well beyond these "pit of despair" emotions, and was even proudly telling my daughter-in-law, Carrie, how far I had progressed. *Where is this coming from? What's going on here?*—I asked myself. *What happened to the "Home is where the Lord Is" state of mind I thought I had graduated to just last week?* This called for a reassessment of my current state. *Have I really been progressing as well as I thought? This is a definite reversal.* Then I got what felt like a revelation.

I paused the movie and went into the kitchen where Carrie was straightening up after dinner. I stood in the doorway and declared to her, "Sandy was everything to me. I'm having trouble moving beyond her." In her usual no-nonsense fashion, Carrie refused to cater to my wallowing in the loss of Sandy. Instead, she said something to the effect of: "Don't do this. Don't allow the pit to swallow you up. Fix your eyes on Jesus. Your future is with Him, not with Sandy. He and He alone can pull you out of despair, set your feet on solid ground, and He will provide a path forward."

While I already knew it, I had to hear that message loud and clear. It translated to, "You have to leave the country of Sandy and move to a new country—the one into which the Lord will lead you." That incident was an important turning point for me. I decided to get a hold of my emotions going forward and reorient my thinking about the country I would now begin occupying.

Processing Sandy's sudden death has been an emotional and mental process. My emotions feel like wild horses. For the most part they are passively grazing in the pasture, causing no trouble. Then, without warning, one takes off running wherever it wants. This is always stirred by a memory of Sandy, triggered by just about anything—such as a family member's suggestion of spaghetti for dinner, reminding me of her amazing spaghetti meat sauce and her asking me to taste it to see if it needs more salt.

Then I'm transported into the kitchen with her, tasting the sauce and telling her it's perfect, nearly as if she's actually there. Seeing her so real and alive in my mind's eye, yet knowing she's gone, is a runaway horse. It's all I can do to hang on. How could the word *spaghetti* have such an emotional impact? Exactly—it shouldn't.

That's when my mental process kicks in. My mind serves as the reins that control my emotional reaction to these triggered moments. I believe that with mental discipline and time (I'm not there yet), I'll be able to keep the horses in the pasture. The horses are memories of Sandy. As long as they are grazing peacefully the memories are sweet, welcome, and enriching. When they take off, with me hanging on, they are hard to round up and they take their toll—sometimes for hours at a time—and can sideline me until they calm down.

While mental discipline is a good tool, that alone isn't enough. Martha W. Hickman is right—at some point I simply need to move on. Move on from preoccupation with thoughts of Sandy that over-dominate my days. Move on from over-referencing her in conversations. Move on from clinging to memories of her in an effort to somehow keep her alive. Move on from the false notion that she is mourning our separation as much as I am.

Moving on also entails believing that life beyond Sandy can be wonderful and rich—and that I will experience joy coming out of grief. This is the hardest part of moving on—acknowledging the possibility that life without Sandy, while different, might be as full and purposeful as the one I had with her. Hard, because on some level I feel as though embracing a bright future is turning my back on, or minimizing, all that I had with her. I spoke of this in the last lesson and Martha W. Hickman addresses it in her *Healing After Loss* entry of September 25:

> A young woman mourning the death of her father said that when she accepted that death was all right, she found within herself a whole new well of energy from which to draw in developing her own life. We may resist such a notion. To ascribe any "benefits" to our loss might imply a diminishment not only of our own sense of loss, but also of the importance of the person we love. If we can get along well without him or her, does it mean the person wasn't as crucial to our life as we had thought?
>
> Not at all. The new energy available to us was formed and nourished in the richness of our relationship with that person. The self that we are will carry our loved one's imprint forever. We have not abandoned him or her any more than he or she has abandoned us. If we find in ourselves a new

maturity, that is part of the person's legacy to us, and he or she would wish us godspeed. But we must be willing to let it happen. I will carry with me forever the strength my loved one bequeathed to me.[9]

So I turn to my new country. Where is it located? What are its borders? How does it differ from the country of Sandy that was such a comfortable home to me for fifty-one years? At this point I can only speak with early forays, glimpses, and intuition, because I have yet to fully inhabit it. But here's what I know so far.

My new country is comprised of a set of experiences which will not include Sandy by my side. These could happen in new places with new people, or with familiar ones experienced alone. The latter includes homes we inhabited together for many years but in which I am now the sole occupant. They include visits with family and close friends where Sandy used to have a prominent place at the table but is now just lovingly remembered.

They include places we used to go together, drives we used to take, movies we used to enjoy, and many other contexts of the life we used to share but I now experience alone. While emotionally harder to navigate than new places with new people, these are unavoidable and need to be incorporated into the fabric of my new country as a solo traveler. Each visit to familiar places or with family and close friends forms a new memory. Over time these memories will take on a life of their own, not replacing those with Sandy but adding to them and changing their landscape.

New places with new people are expanded country borders—those are parts never before traveled with Sandy. These are necessary and important territorial expansions. Recent examples of these include a new apartment in a town closer to my family, to which I'll be moving upon its completion. The building will have other tenants I've never met, who never met Sandy, and with whom I will form relationships.

They also include a Billy Joel concert I attended at Madison Square Garden this summer with our daughter and her close friend; a Broadway show I enjoyed with our daughter and three grandchildren; and a Yankees game I went to with three of our grandchildren. None of these have any Sandy memories associated with them. Each forms the early foundation of a new set of memories I'll be building in this country over the years to come. Each is the start of the infrastructure of my new country. Soon enough there will be new memory highways, bridges, rivers, and buildings.

These are some of the physical attributes of my new country, but there are more substantive ones. And these are where differences with Sandy country are most pronounced. Sandy country was one where the Lord was central—and I'm only just realizing that was due to Sandy.

From the time Sandy would get up in the morning to the time she'd get into bed at night, she would be engaged in studying the Bible (in English and Greek); reading the early church writers works (Clement of Rome, Justin Martyr, Tertullian, Eusebius, and others); and researching and writing articles and books on the ancient church. When she'd finally come into bed, she would place her hand on my head and bless and pray for me before getting into bed. I knew this because I would awaken but pretend to be asleep—so as not to disturb the moment.

On about every level, Sandy loved and enjoyed the Lord throughout the day, and I could tell that He responded by making His presence known in our home. People who visited us would comment on the love and light they sensed. What they were sensing was the Lord's presence.

And what was my contribution to that? Well, I'd like to say it was equal to Sandy's, but it wasn't. My contribution was in loving and tending her as much as I could, being the best husband I could, and supporting her in her study, research, and writing endeavors. I knew what I had in her and wanted to fan her flames of passion for the Lord.

Since Sandy left for heaven, the spiritual attributes of my new country have yet to be defined and formulated. What I know is that they will be markedly different than when she was with me. I'm not a Bible scholar or a historian. I don't read works of the early church fathers. I love the Word, but primarily as a means of daily devotions for setting up my day, and for ensuring that it dwells in me for engagements with friends and strangers throughout the day.

I can't see my study of the Word going much beyond that, and my time with Him in prayer and meditation is limited by my capacity for concentration, which isn't great. In short, I'm no Sandy, and the light of Christ that she illumined in our home feels as if it has been dimmed.

While it won't be the same in my new country, I know the Lord didn't take Sandy out of this world without a plan to compensate for the loss of her making His presence strong in my daily life. I won't be orphaned. So what will it be now? What I'm understanding is that He wants to make His presence known to me more directly, and that I'm in greater need of that now than when Sandy was here—providing me with "air cover," so to speak.

That will entail a new set of habits I haven't yet formed. Mainly, that of spending more time with Him and engaging Him in my comings and goings. Talking with Him about my day, sharing my joys and concerns, and seeking His advice—as one does with a close friend and companion, and as I did with Sandy our whole life.

Sandy was a wonderful listener and counselor. I guess I never felt the need to go much further than her. I miss her terribly in that role but know that I need to turn all that over to the Lord, my new-country life companion. The Lord assures me I won't be disappointed as I transfer that role in my life to Him.

I'm also understanding that one-on-one time with old and new friends will take up a larger part of my weekly schedule. There are few things I enjoy more than listening to people's life stories, sharing my journey, and being a vehicle for the Lord's love, wisdom, and counsel in their lives. That will not require a new set of habits, as it's something I've done since turning my life over to Him in 1970. I just think there will be more opportunities in my future. I have a sense that quite a few of these visits will be with others who have experienced deep loss and just need a friend who understands and has experienced that loss.

Finally, and at the top of my list, I believe I'll spend more time with my children, grandchildren, and their spouses. Sandy was the matriarch of our family, beloved by all for how she brought us together and nurtured us in the Lord. I'm sure her absence in that capacity has left a gaping hole, and with the Lord's help I intend to backfill that to whatever degree possible. She left a great example and imprinted a book of instructions in my heart on how to lead with grace, humility, forgiveness, generosity, encouragement, and unconditional love in all family relationships. My new country will include my best attempts at carrying on her legacy, knowing she would expect nothing less of me.

Reading what I've written here, I like what I see.

I wish this realization was simple. I started this lesson with a description of my partial meltdown during a movie, subsequent need to reassess my grieving progress, and insight that Sandy was my entire country. In reading back over the last several lessons, it's clear that I'm standing with one foot in Sandy country, one in my new country.

Honestly, that's because I loved the Sandy country so much for so long and just don't want it to end. I know the memories will eventually have to supplant the emotional attachments to that country but am now realizing that may take longer that I thought. Some things just can't be rushed. Fortunately, I have the best of all possible journey guides, the Lord Himself, leading the way.

Questions for Reflection

1. Have you come to a point of believing that life without your loved one can still be rich, purposeful, and joyful?

2. Are you held back (from embracing your new country) by preoccupation with thoughts of your former life with your loved one? What are you doing to move on?

3. What are some defining attributes (actual or desired) of your new country?

"AND I PROMISED YOU: YOU WILL INHERIT THEIR LAND, SINCE I WILL GIVE IT TO YOU TO POSSESS, A LAND FLOWING WITH MILK AND HONEY." (LEV. 20:24 CSB)

SEGUE

Grief engulfs us, takes over our lives, renders us impotent. What do we do? Wait. Get through one day. Then another. And another. We feel as though we are only "going through the motions," but it is important to go through the motions. We are, in a strange way, relearning that we are alive. We are alive, functioning, and can do what we need to do. But just barely.

Then one day we're surprised (because how could it be so?) that some of our energy has come back. How did it happen? We didn't expect it, didn't even particularly want it to happen, because we had no expectation of anything happening. The important thing had already passed—the loss of our loved one. But there it is. And our step lightens. And we begin to look around.[10]

I just completed what I have been referring to as my "Segue Tour." Since turning over the keys to the new owners of our Connecticut house, I have been solo-traveling around New England and the Southeast, until arriving at our home in Naples, Florida.

All this travel was to be with family and close friends before starting my new life here in Naples without Sandy. Coming straight to Naples from Connecticut would have been too abrupt. I needed a month of in-depth connection with close and trusted loved ones to build up strength and resolve for reoccupying this all-too-familiar country.

I went to bed early my first night here, slept well, and woke up at peace and ready for this new chapter. Signs of Sandy Country are still everywhere, but these are now more comforting than painful remembrances. As Martha W. Hickman says:

> My step is lightened, and I have begun
> to look around."[11]

However, as our daughter tells me from her own experience of being widowed for five years: "Moving on is not a linear process. Don't expect a switch to go off and every day to be better."

The last two weeks since arriving here have proven this to be the case. On balance, I'm pleasantly surprised by how well my reentry has gone, but there have been periods where memories of Sandy's presence have been so acute that I needed to tighten my seatbelt. When those come, I don't try to deny or push them away. I embrace them while pouring out my love to her and my gratitude to the Lord for the many years He gave me with her, and for the promise that I'll be with her again. As Martha W. Hickman so aptly puts it:

> In the map of the created world, the path to healing does not skirt around the edges of grief but goes right through the middle.[12]

Staying with this analogy of a map of the created world, I'm discovering that my new country is an emerging geographical blend of life on earth without Sandy and anticipation, possibly even foreknowledge, of my future life in heaven. Obviously, life here is my preponderant experience—my feet are planted firmly on this earth. But each day my sense of Sandy's life in heaven becomes incrementally clearer, and I find myself inexplicably sharing in her joy.

To be clear, I'm not in communication with her in heaven, but on some level, I can imagine her life there and that is comforting. My new country entails less missing and longing for her here than being happy for her there. This is a subtle but important difference. Randy Alcorn put it this way in an interview I did with him, wherein we discussed our common experience of the recent loss of our wives, "I have to say that I'm 90 percent rejoicing for Nanci and 10 percent grieving for me. I think that without all the time I've invested in contemplating the wonders of where she is, the proportion would probably be different."

Randy has spent more than twenty years studying, contemplating, and writing about the topic of heaven, on which he has become a leading authority, speaker, and bestselling author. For me, heaven has become a substantive interest only recently (brought on by Sandy's death), so my percentages aren't even close to Randy's. However, I know I'm moving in that direction, and that's good enough for me.

It appears as if the draw of heaven, admittedly intensified by Sandy being there, is causing me to incorporate my future home there into my new country here. I believe those boundary lines will blur over time, and that my final segue will be as simple as walking from one room into another. This insight gives me resolve to, as Sandy used to say, praise my way to victory rather than catalogue my way to defeat. Put another way, less moping and more exalting.

This mindset doesn't mean that I won't continue to have rough waves of missing Sandy, longing for her presence, and wishing I could have her back with me—I do and I will. It also doesn't mean that I won't be lonely for parts of every day lived out without her. I accept these as realties of losing someone as close as she was, and for as long as we were together. It's not that these won't be permanent fixtures, or grief companions as I refer to them. No—it's what I do with them in my new country.

That is where the disciplined mindset of praising my way to victory comes in. Each wave presents a choice— mope or exalt. Cry into the darkness with sadness or cry to the Lord with joy, gratitude, and praise over her inexpressible fulfillment and utter happiness in heaven. Every time I choose praise, my new country becomes more gratifying and the boundaries between earth and heaven become diminished.

Our daughter Kathy, who has become so wise and strong in her five years of grief, always tells me to stay in my lane. This is the lane I will stay in on my new country journey. I may swerve, but I will get back. My new country guide, the Lord, will see to that. This mindset, this lane, will serve me well as I segue to life in my new country.

Questions for Reflection

1. Martha W. Hickman says, "In the map of the created world, the path to healing does not skirt around the edges of grief but goes right through the middle." How would you describe your current position in your journey through grief to your new country?

2. How much of your time would you say you spend being grateful for the new life your loved one is enjoying in heaven versus grieving for yourself? Do you see yourself moving in the right direction?

3. Segue is defined as "a move or shift from one role, state or condition to another." How successfully would you say you are navigating that shift? While grief can't be rushed, what might you do to help the process along?

WEEPING MAY STAY OVERNIGHT, BUT THERE
IS JOY IN THE MORNING. (PS. 30:5 csb)

WHAT WILL I DO TODAY?

I've entered my third week in Naples and am having to deal with a new problem not directly related to grief, but still connected to loss—how to manage all the free time I have now that Sandy is no longer here. Over the twenty-seven years we were together here, we had developed a nice cadence. Filling time was never even a consideration until now.

We were on opposite ends of sleeping schedules. She was a night owl, and I am in bed by 10:00 p.m. I'm an early bird and she slept in most mornings. By the time she was up, I had already had my morning devotional and coffee, and was out and about doing—whatever. I knew she would be at her usual spot in the breakfast room, with morning coffee and Bible, by 10:00 a.m. I would shoot her a text or call just to touch down, let her know what I was up to, and ask when I could pick her up to go to lunch and start our day together.

Starting our day together almost always entailed meeting her outside in the driveway, going to lunch, and my driving her to complete her various shopping errands. I loved being her chauffeur and didn't mind waiting in the car for her to come out of the grocery store or one of her favorite shops. This routine would typically take three hours before going back home.

Sandy's afternoons were hers. That was time for research and writing. She would go into her office, and I knew she was "gone" until evening, when she would be mine again. I would occasionally try to pry her away from her work but was usually unsuccessful. I respected her need for time travel into the ancient world that she so loved, and that took up such a large part of her life from the time she was a young girl. I loved that about her.

During Sandy's private time of research and writing, which usually lasted about four hours, until 7:00 p.m., I would occupy myself in my office or away from the house. It was comforting just knowing she was close by and that I could look forward to our evenings together—and evenings were light, easy, and wonderful. While we had a few close friends we occasionally enjoyed going out with, and certainly did that when family was visiting, most evenings entailed playing cards, bringing dinner in (sometimes she would cook) and watching the news, a movie, or a good period-piece series. We both loved that routine and time flew. We were each other's favorite people. Like I said, filling time was never a consideration.

Of course, all of this changed when Sandy died. The first nine months were occupied with arrangements for her interment and memorial service, frequent family visits, preparing for the sale of our Northern house and relocation closer to our family, and my one-month "segue tour." There was also the first several weeks here of dealing with the aftermath of Hurricane Ian.

But that is all behind me now and I find myself asking, "What will I do today?" The answer isn't obvious. I find myself unenthused about making up golf games (somehow the passion for that has left) and have little to nothing on my schedule to look forward to apart from meeting with a few workers and attending a couple Zoom calls. I'm now making up busy work just to get through the day—and that is unacceptable, so what to do?

What to do?

It's been more than a week since I started this lesson and posed that question. I wanted to wait for an answer before continuing, and I believe I've gotten an inkling of one. I've become increasingly aware that my time is not my own. Like everything else in my possession, that belongs to the Lord. As His servant, I have no more rights to my time than I do to my talents, assets, plans—anything that comprises my life.

I signed all those over to Him when I gave Him my life (which was a mess at the time) in 1970, with Sandy's assistance. That entailed signing over everything to the Lord in return for the promise of a more purposeful life on earth and a future inheritance of eternal life in heaven. That seemed like a great deal at the time—nothing to lose and everything to gain. Over the ensuing fifty-two years since striking that deal (so to speak), the Lord has proven faithful. I have enjoyed an incredibly fruitful, joyful, and purposeful life. Being married to Sandy was central to that.

In retrospect, I was less faithful in keeping my end of the bargain—probably withholding more than I was turning over. However, things have changed. Now that

I'm walking alone with the Lord in my final chapter, I want to hold nothing back—especially my time.

Last night is a good example. After a long afternoon of golf in high heat and humidity, I was exhausted at 6:00 p.m. when I left the club and decided I would go home instead of attending the men's group at my church as intended. A good shower and relaxing dinner watching *The Chosen* seemed like a better alternative. No one would miss me, and I didn't think the Lord would care.

Then I remembered a lunch discussion I had with my pastor a few days before, specifically to discuss how I might fill some of my new-found time with church activities and ministry needs. He recommended getting involved with the weekly men's ministry meeting on Tuesday nights, hence my intention to attend. Knowing that recollection was a prompt by the Lord to follow His answer to prayer, I turned around and went to church, met a bunch of new men, and had a great evening. The right choice.

After I got home, I received two invitations from church friends . . . one for breakfast and the other for a boat ride and lunch—both for this week. I also got a lunch invitation from one of our assistant pastors for lunch next week. As if that wasn't enough to get my attention (that the Lord took me seriously and was taking control of my calendar), I was asked this week if I would be willing to disciple some younger members, assist high school coaches in mentoring students, and correspond with Florida inmates who watch our pastor's sermons and reach out by mail.

My response was an immediate and emphatic yes to all of these invitations. Not "let me think and pray about it, or send me information and I'll consider and get back to you." Like I said above, my time is not my own. And as was the case when I turned my life over to the Lord in 1970, I have nothing to lose and everything to gain.

If Sandy was still alive, I wouldn't have been so quick to agree to take on anything new. I cherished my time with her and increasingly guarded that. I was investing more in our relationship in the last few years than at any other time. I believed then, and still do, that prioritizing time with her in our final chapter of life was the right thing to do. Was that because on some level I knew she would soon be gone? I don't know, but it seemed right, and I sensed the Lord's approval.

Speaking of approval, saying yes to anything and everything the Lord brings to fill my time now that Sandy is in heaven and I'm left here, is exactly what she would want me to do. So the answer to my question is simple—give your time to the Lord and He will fill it.

Questions for Reflection

1. How has your schedule changed since the loss of your loved one?

2. With their absence, are your days longer—and do you find yourself making up busy work just to get through the day? What ways can you change your current schedule to help move forward into your new country?

3. Do you consider your time your own, or the Lord's to do with as He pleases and directs? Have you given your time to Him? If so, how is that going? If not, what practical things can you do to reorient your time to be less boring and more purposeful?

**PAY CAREFUL ATTENTION, THEN,
TO HOW YOU WALK—NOT AS UNWISE
PEOPLE BUT AS WISE—MAKING THE MOST
OF THE TIME. (EPH. 5:15–16 CSB)**

THE VIBRANCY OF MEMORIES

Deeper and deeper we burrow into our grief. Desolations pile on one another. We wonder if we shall ever see anything on the horizon but this gloom and sadness. Then one day, in some moment of quiet reflection, we find ourselves Thinking of Something Else! Is it possible?

We will move back and forth many times—back into the dark woods and forward again into the light. After a while we will realize it is all one world, that feelings of joy and sadness enrich each other—as a person who has been totally ill has a new appreciation for the beauty of starlight, the taste of orange juice, the caress of love.[13]

Reading Martha Hickman's devotional this morning helped me understand the sadness-and-joy tug-of-war I've been wrestling with. As is often the case, Martha is able to tell me what I'm experiencing because she's been through it—like an expert guide who knows the terrain. That's the way it is with grief sojourners. We share a common bond and benefit from those who have walked in our shoes.

It is eleven months tomorrow since Sandy's death, and I can say with certainty that joy is now the prevailing emotion in my "new country" life. This is a significant transition. I go to bed at peace, awaken looking forward to the day ahead, and have transferred my companion dependence to the Lord. I still miss Sandy every day but my "relationship" with her has changed—it has moved into new territory, best described in the text I sent to our older son last night:

> My relationship with Mom is changing
> from the one I had with her before to
> the one I have with her now in sweet
> memories. This is a veiled mystery, but
> I trust the Lord to put it all in perspec-
> tive in His time.

It may seem strange to speak in terms of a relationship with a loved one who has passed. "Relationship" implies interaction and communication. I no longer have that with Sandy, but bits and pieces of the interactions we had for fifty-one years roll through my head daily as fond and familiar reminiscences. They will always be a part of me, as will the memory of her warmth, smiles, embraces—her "Sandyness."

Yes, they bring me to tears but with a smile—no longer longing as much for her physical presence but content with and grateful for the vibrancy of memories. The vibrancy of memories. I love the sound of that.

What would we do without our good memories? They feed our souls and help make us the people we are. I am one who has been blessed with a lifetime of fond memories—mainly comprised of those made with Sandy and our family.

Of course, being human and living in a fallen world, there are also unpleasant memories. Some of mine are of times when I was unkind to her—when I was proud, defensive, and childish. Times when I caused her to go into her shell to protect herself from a man she didn't recognize, and when I needed to coax her out with apologies for my foolishness.

I'm happy to say those were rare in the last ten years of our marriage. While I wish they had never occurred, they were always quickly resolved with grace and forgiveness. That was the way it was with us. Grace and forgiveness always prevailed. When she looked at me with sad and loving eyes, saying goodbye just before closing them to leave for heaven—I know there wasn't a trace of anything other than memories of the wonderful love and life we shared.

A few weeks ago I was feeling sorry and guilty about times I was unkind to her—memories creeping in to steal my joy. I called our daughter-in-law to rehash them. She was quick to ask if I was re-litigating times that were forgiven, over and done with. I admitted that I was, and her answer was predicable—would Sandy want you to dredge those up? Would the Lord? Is forgiveness not really forgiveness?

That was what I needed to hear. I won't allow 10 percent of regrets to cloud 90 percent of beautiful memories.

So what is the role of fond memories of our loved one in living a full and joyful life? For me they serve as ballasts that keep my earth-bound ship steady. Knowing that our love is an eternal gift to be continued when we are reunited in heaven, vibrant memories of her are reminders of that promise.

Her physical presence with me on earth left, but the memories of our life together didn't die when she did. In fact, they have become more alive. Earlier in my grief process I attempted to quench them because they painfully punctuated her death. Now I cherish, welcome, and encourage them as proxies for a new and even better relationship that has yet to be revealed.

They fuel my joy.

Questions for Reflection

1. Grief can manifest as a tug-of-war of emotions between sadness over the painful loss of our loved one and joy from the vibrant and wonderful memories of our life with them—and anticipation of being reunited in heaven. Which side of you is winning that tug-of-war? What can you do to give the advantage to vibrant memories and hopeful anticipation?

2. "Relationship" with a loved one implies physical interaction and communication, but there are also the memories—bits and pieces of daily interactions as fond and familiar reminiscences. These constitute a reformulation of our "relationship." Have you been able to transition to that state of mind? How can you transition your relationship with your memories to be one that brings you joy?

3. Not all memories are good ones. There were times when we were unkind, proud, and far less than Christlike in our behavior toward our loved one. Hopefully you asked forgiveness for those times. However, if you didn't it's not too late to bring your guilt over these to the Lord and ask His forgiveness. He doesn't want unpleasant memories to pock your current and future joy. Have you done that?

**I WILL THANK THE LORD WITH ALL MY HEART;
I WILL DECLARE ALL YOUR WONDROUS
WORKS. (PS. 9:1 CSB)**

CHOOSE TO CHERISH

> We are the best judges of when to stay in our grief and when to move on to something else. The important thing is to inwardly accept responsibility for the choices we make. And to recognize the difference between grieving over the loss of a loved one and continuing to cherish that person.[14]

Recognize the difference between grieving over the loss of a loved one and continuing to cherish that person. For me, this is a profound statement that defines the inflection point I've entered on this one-year anniversary of Sandy's death.

I can choose to stay stuck in the gear of grief as the center of my life—constantly grieving over the loss of her—or shift gears to cherishing her. Cherish the person she was here. Cherish the millions of moments we shared over our fifty-one years together. Cherish the slideshow of her face, smile, and voice, which plays through my head daily. Cherish the thoughts of her new life in heaven and of our future reunion there.

Cherishing is not worshipping. I worship the Lord but cherish the gift of Sandy—as one does something priceless. Sandy was a gift I didn't deserve and wasn't worthy of. I always knew that, was constantly amazed by it, but came to accept the gift with gratitude. She was, quite simply, beyond me on every level—but she fell in love with and gave her heart and soul to me. I did my best to prove worthy of that and remained faithful to her love and trust. I cherish the fact that I can say that with impunity (a word Sandy loved).

So, as I move into year two, I choose to cherish Sandy. That will be the theme of my thoughts toward her. Grief has indeed been my friend over this past year. It has allowed me to pour out tears of sadness over her loss, cleanse my soul, and transform me into a better man than I otherwise would have been without the depths to which it took me. However, cherishing the gift of her will be the substance of my reflections on Sandy from now on.

Questions for Reflection

1. We can control whether to stay stuck in the gear of sadness (over the loss of our loved one) or to shift gears to cherishing the sweet memories of the life we shared with them. Which gear are you currently in?

2. Are you able to recognize the difference between continuously grieving over the loss of your loved one and joyfully cherishing them in your heart?

3. It is possible to feel possessive of our grief. In this sense, our grief could become an idol. When have you seen yourself falling into the trap of worshipping your grief?

WE DO NOT WANT YOU TO BE UNINFORMED, BROTHERS AND SISTERS, CONCERNING THOSE WHO ARE ASLEEP, SO THAT YOU WILL NOT GRIEVE LIKE THE REST, WHO HAVE NO HOPE. FOR IF WE BELIEVE THAT JESUS DIED AND ROSE AGAIN, IN THE SAME WAY, THROUGH JESUS, GOD WILL BRING WITH HIM THOSE WHO HAVE FALLEN ASLEEP. (1 THESS. 4:13–14 csb)

OUT OF THE NEST

In the midst of the deepest winter, of the darkest night, what are we to do? Acknowledge the cold and the dark, the mystery of an unknowable black ocean that seems to stretch into infinity . . . and then sing! Or to put it another way, "it is better to light a candle than curse the darkness." One of the glories of human beings is their ability to venture, to see beyond the immediate scene, to raise a note of hope and risk in a sometimes foreboding world.

So may this New Year's Eve—this turning into the next year, this milestone which has its aura of sadness because I enter another year without my loved one—may this New Year's Eve be for me a time for music. And if I am able—later, if not now—may I hear in my heart the voice of my loved one lifted with my voice, to praise life, to hope for life, to join others in this circling globe in an "Alleluia," for the experiences we have shared and share even now, and for the ways beyond time and death in which we are bound to one another in gratitude and love.[15]

In reading over the preceding lessons, I can see that I'm now out of the nest, so to speak. I have made numerous attempts, only to return to the nest, where I lingered close to Sandy—home base. I was reluctant to leave, finding comfort and security in the shadow of her presence, but that is no longer necessary nor a healthy way to live out the rest of my life. In my mind I imagine Sandy instructing me to fly.

> *Fly, Honey.*
> *There is so much to see, do, and live for. You are strong in the Lord and ready to continue on your own. I will be exploring my new country while you explore yours. And then, one glorious day you will fly to me—where we will explore heaven for eternity. And what a day that will be. I have always loved you and can hardly wait to be with you again.*

> Fly, Honey.

Sandy's Christ-centered wisdom always served me well. How many times I would have veered off the road and into a ditch, only to be pulled back by her. While I still drive over curbs a lot, my car stays on the road, and I can find my way around without her by my side.

The Lord has taken her place next to me and speaks to me through His Word: "For I know the plans I have for you," declares the LORD, "plans to prosper you and not to harm you, plans to give you hope and a future" (Jer. 29:11). While I haltingly fly, the Lord smiles and tells me, "Sandy is in My care, as are you—stay close to Me and I won't let you fall—all will be well."

And all indeed is well. The man I have become through this ordeal is better than the one I was before—broken, and thus more tender, sensitive to others, and appreciative of the simple things around me. Of course, I'd prefer that Sandy hadn't had her accident and died a year ago, but this reshaping of the man who will carry on is the silver lining. Nothing is lost with God. All things work together for good when we turn our joys and sorrows, gains and losses over to Him.

I will finish this lesson with a quote from Martha W. Hickman, who has walked beside me through her writing and given voice to my own journey through grief. Here she describes exactly where I am as I turn the page and occupy my new country.

> Back when our grief was fresh, we thought this would never happen— that we would take pleasure in the small, ordinary events of life. Back then, we thought our perception of the world would always be dominated by this piercing, overriding loss. So, we're twice blessed when, a bit at a

time, we begin to savor once more the lovely ongoing processes by which life is quietly fostered, day by day.

We're twice blessed because the sharp teeth of our loss no longer bite into our consciousness all the time, and because we're aware of the wonderful life sustaining things going on around us—like red cardinals against winter snow or the warmth of fire when we have come in from the cold. We used to take these for granted. Then nothing was to be taken for granted anymore. And now perhaps we—even we—can relax into the everyday and begin to trust life again.[16]

Questions for Reflection

1. Our grief can, in a way, become the "nest" to which we return to feel closer to the loved one we lost but who, alas, is no longer there. On one level that can be a comforting temporary abode, but it is not our new country to be explored and occupied. Do you find yourself lingering too long in the nest of grief? What are you doing to increase your flight time away?

2. The nineteenth-century English evangelist J. C. Ryle (1816–1900) describes abiding in Christ as: "Always leaning on Him, resting on Him, pouring out our hearts to Him, and using Him as our Fountain of life and strength, as our chief Companion and best Friend." Have you begun forays into this (more perfect) place of abiding? If not, try asking the Lord to help you get there. He most assuredly will.

"AS THE FATHER HAS LOVED ME, I HAVE ALSO LOVED YOU. REMAIN (ABIDE) IN MY LOVE. IF YOU KEEP MY COMMANDS YOU WILL REMAIN IN MY LOVE, JUST AS I HAVE KEPT MY FATHER'S COMMANDS AND REMAIN IN HIS LOVE. I HAVE TOLD YOU THESE THINGS SO THAT MY JOY MAY BE IN YOU AND YOUR JOY MAY BE COMPLETE." (JOHN 15:9–11 CSB)

I DON'T HAVE TO BE ALONE

After an appropriate period of time, friends and acquaintances began asking me if I was open to dating or even remarrying. This was always done with care and respect. Up until recently, my immediate answer was "no." I couldn't imagine a scenario where I would be open to allowing another woman into the space that had been occupied exclusively by Sandy. I was certain I would be content to live the rest of my life with sweet memories of her and able to fill my loneliness void with the Lord, family, and friends.

Then something happened. The clock moved to eighteen months following Sandy's death and a window opened—one to receptivity of sharing my life with someone besides Sandy. Not someone who would replace her, but someone with whom I could share life in a special way. Someone I could think about and communicate with throughout the day. Someone I could care for and be cared for by beyond a casual friendship. Someone with whom I could be comfortable, relaxed, compatible, and able to share interests and affection.

It's difficult to define the boundaries of companionship and romance in this would-be relationship. I'm open to either, depending on what the Lord has in mind for me. At the moment, there is only the possibility of someone to fill the loneliness. What I'm fairly certain of is that I don't have to be alone. I know the Lord will lead me to someone whose needs are similar to mine, who loves Him, and who is seeking His direction for someone special. I'm good with that.

I'm glad to be ending on such a happy and hopeful note.

They say grief can't be rushed, and that no two people process it the same. For me, it has been the most challenging and life-changing experience I have ever had. It has turned me upside down, inside out, and reoriented my priorities, relationships, and attitudes toward what is and isn't important

I attribute this phenomenon to being taken apart by the upheaval of losing my other half, and being put back together as a different person—without Sandy in person, but with her in vibrant memories still developing and taking shape. While grief has not ended for me after eighteen months, a significant positive shift has taken place. I can see a wonderful transformation underway.

I have turned over this transformation process to the Lord and asked Him to discard everything that shouldn't make the journey. We don't want useless or excess baggage that would be inadmissible in heaven.

This new country is shaping up to be a welcome and exciting stopover to my ultimate destination. Until that time, I plan on living this life to the fullest with the Lord guiding every step.

I am not alone—and neither are you! Every person's journey through grief is different. Your process is not going to look the same as mine. You may travel faster or slower or have more U-turns. You may have read some of these lessons and thought, *I'll never get to that point*, but I hope that regardless of our differences, that these lessons have been signposts for you. Landmarks along the path marked by a fellow traveler to remind you that while we may travel our paths in different ways, we are not the only ones who have made the journey, and throughout it all, the Lord has been by each of our sides.

Questions for Reflection

1. Those in grief experience loneliness in different ways and in varying degrees. In my case, loneliness has been one of the greatest trials with which I have had to contend. Has this been a significant problem for you? How have you dealt with your loneliness?

2. Rather than letting yourself feel trapped in isolation, who are the people that God has placed around you to remind you that you are not alone, and to help you fill the void?

3. If you recently lost your spouse, are you open to the possibility of entering into a companionship or love relationship with someone else? What do you consider to be the boundaries of such a relationship, and how far would you be willing to take it—Just friendship? Borderline romance? Marriage?

THEN THE Lord GOD SAID, "IT IS NOT GOOD FOR THE MAN TO BE ALONE. I WILL MAKE A HELPER (A COMPANION) CORRESPONDING TO HIM." (GEN. 2:18 CSB)

ACKNOWLEDGMENTS

To my close friends and family who encouraged me to start a grief journal after my wife's passing. Originally intended for grappling with and healing from my sudden loss, the journal morphed into this book of lessons learned. It was their moving responses to the lessons that inspired me to seek a publisher to share them with an audience of fellow grief sojourners.

You were there for me in my darkest hours, listened to me read my work in progress through shared tears, provided loving counsel and support, and celebrated the publication of this book with me. In short, this would not have been possible without you. You know who you are.

To my publisher Mary Wiley and editor Clarissa Dufresne at Lifeway/B&H who believed in this book's ability to minister Christ's love and healing into the lives of those needing a friend who could share their grief and provide hope and consolation.

To Martha W. Hickman, now deceased and reunited with the daughter she tragically lost at the age of sixteen, who through her book *Healing After Loss*, was so meaningful and helpful to me in my first year of grief. I have included extracts from Martha's book throughout mine, as she often expresses best what I'm trying to say.

Finally, to you my reader, for allowing me to come along side you in your grief. It is my prayer that our time together here will help you find the hope, joy, peace, and new county that surely awaits you.

—Stephen Silver

NOTES

1. Randy Alcorn, *Heaven: A Comprehensive Guide to Everything the Bible Says about Our Eternal Home* (Carol Stream, IL: Tyndale House, 2004), 336–37.

2. Twitter, March 28, 2022, @randyalcorn, https://x.com/randyalcorn/status/1508573673170505729?s=20

3. Robert Jeffress, *A Place Called Heaven: 10 Surprising Truths about Your Eternal Home* (Grand Rapids, MI: Baker Books, 2018).

4. Martha W. Hickman, *Healing After Loss: Meditations for Working through Grief* (New York: Avon Books, 1994), July 27.

5. Tim Keller, *Prayer: Experiencing Awe and Intimacy with God* (New York, Penguin, 2014), 232.

6. Martha W. Hickman, *Healing After Loss: Meditations for Working through Grief* (New York: Avon Books, 1994), August 15.

7. Hickman, *Healing After Loss*, August 18.

8. Hickman, *Healing After Loss*.

9. Hickman, *Healing After Loss*, September 25.

10. Martha W. Hickman, *Healing After Loss*, October 10.

11. Hickman, *Healing After Loss*.

12. Hickman, *Healing After Loss*.

13. Hickman, *Healing After Loss*, November 11.

14. Hickman, *Healing After Loss*, November 22.

15. Hickman, *Healing After Loss*, December 31.

16. Hickman, *Healing After Loss*, December 6.